BREATHING
THE WATER

Books by Denise Levertov

Poetry

The Double Image

Here and Now

Overland to the Islands

With Eyes at the Back of Our Heads

The Jacob's Ladder

O Taste and See

The Sorrow Dance

Relearning the Alphabet

To Stay Alive

Footprints

The Freeing of the Dust

Life in the Forest

Collected Earlier Poems 1940–1960

Candles in Babylon

Poems 1960–1967

Oblique Prayers

Poems 1968–1972

Breathing the Water

Prose

The Poet in the World

Light Up the Cave

Translations

Guillevic/Selected Poems

BREATHING THE WATER

DENISE LEVERTOV

A NEW DIRECTIONS BOOK

Grateful acknowledgment is made to the editors and publishers of magazines in which some of the poems in this collection previously appeared: *The Agni Review, Articles, Five Fingers Review, KSOR Guide, Michigan Quarterly Review, North American Review, Open Places, Poetry East, Poetry Kanto* (Japan), *Radcliffe Quarterly, Religion & Intellectual Life, The Rialto* (England), *Sequoia, Sojourners, Southern Humanities Review,* and *Wisconsin Review.*

"Caedmon" originally appeared as a broadside (William B. Ewert, Publisher). The following poems were originally published in limited editions: "Urgent Whisper," "During a Son's Dangerous Illness," and "Carapace" as *The Menaced World* (William B. Ewert, Publisher); the poems of both groups of "Spinoffs" as *Spinoffs* (Copper Canyon Press). The first group of "Spinoffs" will be included in the forthcoming portfolio of Peter McAfee Brown's photographs.

The epigraph is taken from "Music from Spain," in *The Golden Apples,* copyright 1949, 1977 by Eudora Welty. Reprinted by permission of Harcourt Brace Jovanovich, Inc.

Manufactured in the United States of America.
First published clothbound and as New Directions Paperback 640 in 1987
Published simultaneously in Canada by Penguin Books Canada Limited

Library of Congress Cataloging-in-Publication Data
Levertov, Denise, 1923–
   Breathing the water.
   (A New Directions Book)
   I. Title.
PS3562.E8876B7   1987   811'.54   86–23658
ISBN 0–8112–1026–X
ISBN 0–8112–1027–8 (pbk.)

New Directions Books are published for James Laughlin
by New Directions Publishing Corporation
80 Eighth Avenue, New York 10011

Contents

"Was it so strange, the way things are flung out at us, like the apples of Atlanta perhaps, once we have begun a certain onrush?"

Eudora Welty,
"Music from Spain,"
The Golden Apples

I

Variation on a Theme by Rilke

(The Book of Hours, *Book I, Poem 1, Stanza 1*)

A certain day became a presence to me;
there it was, confronting me—a sky, air, light:
a being. And before it started to descend
from the height of noon, it leaned over
and struck my shoulder as if with
the flat of a sword, granting me
honor and a task. The day's blow
rang out, metallic—or it was I, a bell awakened,
and what I heard was my whole self
saying and singing what it knew: *I can.*

3

Leaf through discolored manuscripts,
make sure no words
lie thirsting, bleeding,
waiting for rescue. No:
old loves half-
articulated, moments forced
out of the stream of perception
to play 'statue',
and never released—
they had no blood to shed.
You must seek
the ashy nest itself
if you hope to find
charred feathers, smouldering flightbones,
and a twist of singing flame
rekindling.

Slowly the crows patrol the parapet.
A leopard-slug, sated with leaf-juice, vanishes for the day.
Brown, untwirling, laburnum seedpods recapitulate
the golden rain of June.
                              Indoors, the timid millipedes
venture a tango across the cellar floor.
I hear the books in all the rooms
breathing calmly, and remember a dream I had years ago:
my father—all that complexity, cabalistic lore,
childish vanity, heroic wisdom, goodness, weakness,
defeat and faith—had become, after traveling
through death's gated tunnel, a rose,
                    an old-fashioned dark-pink garden rose.

There is no breeze. A milky sky. Traces
of blue shadow
                    melting like ice.
The day will be hot.
Not shadow—wisps of night. I feel them
under my eyes; and after a deep breath
at the open window, draw down the blind.
It meant, I say to myself, he let knowledge
                    fall from his hands,
no longer needed: now he could be his essence,
            it was there all along, many-petaled, fragrant,
'a blissful foolish rose' in the sun.
                    I return to sleep
as if to the slippery fragrance
of pinewoods, the needles' shelving
in soft darkness, the last of night
retrieved.

A Blessing

For Joanna Macy

'Your river is in full flood,' she said,
'Work on—use these weeks well!'
She was leaving, with springy step, a woman
herself renewed, her life risen
up from the root of despair she'd
bent low to touch,
risen empowered. Her work now
could embrace more: she imagined anew
the man's totem tree and its taproot,
the woman's chosen lichen, patiently
composting rock, another's
needful swamp, the tribal migrations—
swaying skeins rotating their leaders,
pace unflagging—and the need
of each threatened thing
to be. She had met
with the *council*
of all beings.

                            'You give me
my life,' she said to the just-written poems,
long-legged foals surprised to be standing.

The poet waving farewell
is not so sure of the river.
Is it indeed
strong-flowing, generous? Was there largesse
for alluvial, black, seed-hungry fields?
Or had a flash-flood
swept down these tokens
to be plucked ashore, rescued
only to watch the waters recede
from stones of an arid valley?

But the traveler's words
are leaven. They work in the poet.
The river swiftly
goes on braiding its heavy tresses,
brown and flashing,
as far as the eye can see.

A wanderer comes at last
to the forest hut where it was promised
someone wise would receive him.
And there's no one there; birds and small animals
flutter and vanish, then return to observe.
No human eyes meet his.
But in the hut there's food,
set to keep warm beside glowing logs,
and fragrant garments to fit him, replacing
the rags of his journey,
and a bed of heather from the hills.
He stays there waiting. Each day the fire
is replenished, the pot refilled while he sleeps.
He draws up water from the well,
writes of his travels, listens for footsteps.
Little by little he finds
the absent sage is speaking to him,
is present.

                      This is the way
you have spoken to me, the way—startled—
I find I have heard you. When I need it,
a book or a slip of paper
appears in my hand, inscribed by yours: messages
waiting on cellar shelves, in forgotten boxes
until I would listen.

                    Your spirits relax;
now she is looking, you say to each other,
now she begins to see.

II

SPINOFFS, ONE

   . . . And light made of itself an amber
transparency one sundown, restoring
Moorish atavistic imprints almost
to memory, patterns tight-closed
eyes used to make in childhood when
the greenish thickwoven cotton tablecover,
frayed and become an ironing sheet, linked itself somehow
to a Septembery casbah imagined
before any casbah became knowledge . . .

Tempered wood. Wrought light. Carved
rags. Curdled gold, the thin
sheets of it. The leaves of it.
The wet essence of it infused.
Effluvia of gold suffused throughout. The saturation.
The drying. The flaking. The absorption.
It is a paper sack, a paper sack for dogfood, dry,
the dry wafers of a sacrament, a sacred sack,
its brownish pallor illumined, inscribed with red,
upheld by a many-layered substance
plush as moss, chocolate-dark, dense, which is shadow,
and backed by a tentative, a tremulous
evanescence which is wood
or which is the tardy sungleam from under cloudbank
just before evening settles,
that percolates through cobwebs and thick glass.
Which is the fleeting conjugation
of wood and light, embrace that leaves wood
dizzy and insubstantial, and leaves light
awestruck again at its own destiny.

Much happens when we're not there.
Many trees, not only that famous one, over and over,
fall in the forest. We don't see, but something sees,
or someone, a different kind of someone,
a different molecular model, or entities
not made of molecules anyway; or nothing, no one:
but something has taken place, taken space,
                              been present, absent,
returned. Much moves in and out of open windows
when our attention is somewhere else,
just as our souls move in and out of our bodies sometimes.
Everyone used to know this,
but for a hundred years or more
we've been losing our memories, moulting, shedding,
like animals or plants that are not well.
Things happen anyway,
whether we are aware or whether
the garage door comes down by remote control over our
recognitions, shuts off, cuts off—.
We are animals and plants that are not well.
We are not well but while we look away,
on the other side of that guillotine or through
the crack of day disdainfully left open below the blind
a very strong luminous arm reaches in,
or from an unsuspected place, in the room with us,
where it was calmly waiting, reaches outward.
And though it may have nothing at all to do with us,
and though we can't fathom its designs,
nevertheless our condition thereby changes:
cells shift, a rustling barely audible as of tarlatan
flickers through closed books, one or two leaves
fall, and when we read them we can perceive,
if we are truthful, that we were not dreaming,
not dreaming but once more witnessing.

Everything was very delicately striped.
You could see the wood-pulse exquisitely throb
under paint's thin tissue, beside
the mirror limpid in its film
of silver,
most justly beveled,
most faintly steam-blurred,
most faintly warped as if with just sufficient
bruise to tinge
with tenderness its icy patience.
A few sheets of paper were still on the roll;
the austere and efficient holder cast, in the shadows,
a sprightly fantasy of itself in stronger shadow, crossing
the beveled molding. This the glass
never could reflect,
never unless the entire closet door, wrenched from its hinges,
were placed across the room and
forced to look back,
or a second mirror
brought in to face it: neither of them
with a word to say.
There was blue, there was brown paler than ivory,
                              a half-curtain,
there were other blues and an aspiration to whiteness,
there were preludes to green, pink, gold and aluminum,
mostly there was the sense that though
the light would fade
and return next day and slowly move
from right to left and again
fade and return, yet
the stillness here, so delicate,
pulse unquickened, could outwait
every move.

The wind behind the window moves the leaves.

James with his cockleshell or Genevieve
a fraction westward move each day
in ruby beads,

a rosary let fall (*with lily, germander, and sops-in-wine*)
decade by decade through the year
across the wall, along the floor.

The figures ripple and the colors quicken.
In cloud or dark invisible
yet moving always, and in light

turning—the circle
east by west or west by east
day after day

constant in pilgrimage. The wind
behind the window moves
the leaves, the bare

branches stir or hold
their breath, their buds,
up to remotest stars.

And dustmote congregations file
endlessly through the slanted amethyst.

III

'I am a landscape,' he said,
'a landscape and a person walking in that landscape.
There are daunting cliffs there,
and plains glad in their way
of brown monotony. But especially
there are sinkholes, places
of sudden terror, of small circumference
and malevolent depths.'
'I know,' she said. 'When I set forth
to walk in myself, as it might be
on a fine afternoon, forgetting,
sooner or later I come to where sedge
and clumps of white flowers, rue perhaps,
mark the bogland, and I know
there are quagmires there that can pull you
down, and sink you in bubbling mud.'
'We had an old dog,' he told her, 'when I was a boy,
a good dog, friendly. But there was an injured spot
on his head, if you happened
just to touch it he'd jump up yelping
and bite you. He bit a young child,
they had to take him down to the vet's and destroy him.'
'No one knows where it is,' she said,
'and even by accident no one touches it.
It's inside my landscape, and only I, making my way
preoccupied through my life, crossing my hills,
sleeping on green moss of my own woods,
I myself without warning touch it,
and leap up at myself—'
'—or flinch back
just in time.'
            'Yes, we learn that.
It's not terror, it's pain we're talking about:
those places in us, like your dog's bruised head,
that are bruised forever, that time
never assuages, never.'

19

Uninterpreted, the days
are falling.

The spring wind
is shaking and shaking the trees.

A nest of eggs,
a nest of deaths.

Falling
abandoned.

The palms rattle, the eucalypts
shed bark and blossom. Uninterpreted.

This morning's morning-glory
trying to thrust
through the wire mesh towards the sun
is trapped
        half-open.
I ease it back
to see better its unfurling,

but only slowly it resigns
the dream. Its petals
are scarred.
I had not thought myself
a jailor.

A greyish bird
the size perhaps of two plump sparrows,
fallen in some field,
soon flattened, a dry
mess of feathers—
and no one knows
this was a prince among his kind,
virtuoso of virtuosos,
lord of a thousand songs,
debonair, elaborate in invention, fantasist,
rival of nightingales.

In Memory: After a Friend's Sudden Death

(A.N., 1943–1985)

Others will speak of her spirit's tendrils reaching
almost palpably into the world;

but I will remember her body's unexpected beauty
seen in the fragrant redwood sauna,

young, vestal, though she was nearing fifty
and had borne daughters and a son—

a 15th century widehipped grace,
small waist and curving belly,

breasts with that look
of inexhaustible gentleness,
shoulders narrow but strong.

And I will speak
not of her work, her words, her search
for a new pathway, her need

to heedfully walk and sing through dailiness
noticing stones and flowers,

but of the great encompassing *Aah!* she would utter,
entering slowly, completely, into the welcoming whirlpool.

Missing Beatrice

(For B.H., 1944–1985)

Goodness was
a fever in you. Anyone

might glow in the heat of it,
go home comforted—

for them a shawl, for you
fire at the bone.

•

You knew
more than was good for you.
Your innocence
was peat-bog water, subtle and dark,
that cold it was,
that pure.

•

Kindness—didn't we act as though
we could cut an endless supply from you
like turf from a bog?

•

Smoke of that empty hearth
fragrant still.
Your words
cupped in our hands to drink.
But you—
you're gone and we never
really saw you.

24

When the last sunlight had all seeped
down behind the woods and taken
colors and shadows with it, leaving us
not in darkness but in
the presence of an absence, with everything
still visible but
empty of soul—

when we trudged on knowing our home was
miles and hours away and the real dark
overtaking us, and mother and father waiting
anxious by now and soon
growing angry because again
we'd traveled too far out and away, leaving
almost as if
not to return—

what did you, almost grown up, feel
as we spoke less and less, too tired
for fantasy? I was afraid for them,
for their fear and of
its show of anger, but not of the night.
I felt the veil
of sadness descend

but I was never afraid for us,
we were benighted but not lost, and I trusted
utterly that at last,
however late, we'd get home.
No owl, no lights, the dun ridges
of ploughland fading. No matter.
I trusted you.

But you? Irritably you'd ask me
why I was silent. Was it because
you felt untrusted, or had no trust
in yourself? Could it,
could it have been that
you, you were afraid,
my brave, my lost
sister?

The ash tree drops the few dry leaves it bore in May,
stands naked by mid-July.
When each day's evil news drains into the next,
a monotonous overflow,
has a tree's dying lost the right to be mourned?
No—life's indivisible. And this tree,
rooted beyond my fence, has been,
branch and curved twig, in leaf or bare, the net
that held the sky in my window.
Trunk in deep shade, its lofting crown
offers to each long day's
pale glow after the sun
is almost down, an answering gold—
the last light
held and caressed.

Three men spoke to me today.

One, bereaved, told me his grief, saying
Had God abandoned him, or was there
no God to abandon him?

One, condemned, told me his epitaph,
'Groomed to die.' On Death Row he remembers
the underside of his gradeschool desk, air-raid drill.
He never expected to live
even this long.
He sticks his head back down between his knees,
'not even sad.'

One, a young father, told me
how he had needed his child, even
before she was conceived.
How he had planted a garden too big to hoe.
He told me about the small leaves near his window,
how he had seen in them their desire to be,
to be the world.

With this one I sat laughing,
eating, drinking wine. 'The same word,'
he said, 'she has the same word for me and the dog!
She loves us!'

Every day, every day I hear
enough to fill
a year of nights with wondering.

Nail the rose
           to your mind's door
like a rat, a thwarted chickenhawk.
Yes, it has had its day.

And the water
           poured for you
which you disdain to drink,
yes, throw it away.

Yet the fierce rose
           stole nothing
from your cooped heart,
nor plucked your timid eye;

and from inviolate rock
           the liquid light
was drawn, that's dusty now
and your lips dry.

IV

The Wishing Well was a spring
bubbling clear and soundless into a shallow pool
less than three feet across, a hood of rocks
protecting it, smallest of grottoes, from falling leaves,
the pebbles of past wishes peacefully under-water, old desires
forgotten or fulfilled. No one threw money in, one had to search
for the right small stone.

This was the place from which
year after year in childhood I demanded my departure,
my journeying forth into the world of magical
cities, mountains, otherness—the place which gave
what I asked, and more; to which
still wandering, I returned this year, as if
to gaze once more at the face
of an ancient grandmother.
And I found the well
filled to the shallow brim
with debris of a culture's sickness—
with bottles, tins, paper, plastic—
the soiled bandages
of its aching unconsciousness.

Does the clogged spring still moisten
the underlayer of waste?
Was it children threw in the rubbish?
Children who don't dream, or dismiss
their own desires and
toss them down, discarded packaging?
I move away, walking fast, the impetus
of so many journeys pushes me on,
but where are the stricken children of this time, this place,
to travel to, in Time if not in Place,
the grandmother wellspring choked, and themselves not aware
of all they are doing-without?

You could die before me—
I've known it
always, the
dreaded worst, 'unnatural' but
possible
in the play
of matter, matter and
growth and
fate.

·

My sister Philippa died
twelve years before I was born—
the perfect, laughing firstborn,
a gift to be cherished as my orphaned mother
had not been cherished. Suddenly:
death, a baby

cold and still.

·

Parent, child—death ignores
protocol, a sweep of its cape brushes
this one or that one at random
into the dust, it was
not even looking.
                What becomes
of the past if the future
snaps off, brittle,
the present left as a jagged edge
opening on nothing?

·

Grief for the menaced world—lost rivers,
poisoned lakes—all creatures, perhaps,
to be fireblasted
                    off the
whirling cinder we
loved, but not enough . . .
The grief I'd know if I
lived into
your unthinkable death
is a splinter
of that selfsame grief,
infinitely smaller but
the same in kind:
one
stretching the mind's fibers to touch
eternal nothingness,
the other
tasting, in fear, the
desolation of
survival.

I am growing mine
though I have regretted yours.

> She says, Sure I saw him: he wanted
> to run, the Guardia Civil
> shot him before he reached the patio wall.
> Do I understand 'subversive'? Yes,
> the word means
> people who know their rights,
> if they work but don't get enough to eat
> they protest. He was
> a lay preacher, my father,
> he preached the Gospel,
> he was subversive.

> She is 12.

My shell is growing
nicely, not very hard, just
a thin protection but it's
better than just skin. Have you
completed yours? It seems
there will be chinks in it though,
the cartilaginous
plates don't quite meet, do yours?

> A 9 year old boy whose father has 'disappeared'
>   three weeks now,
> asked how he feels, says
> with the shrug of a man of sixty,
> 'sad.' He nods. 'Yes; sad . . .'

That burning, blistering glare
off the world's desert
still pushes in; oh, filter it, grow faster,
hide me in shadow,
     my carapace!

It could be the râle of Earth's tight chest,
her lungs scarred from old fevers, and she asleep—

but there's no news from the seismographs,
the crystal pendant
hangs plumb from its hook;

and yet at times (and I whisper because
it's a fearful thing I tell you)
a subtle shudder has passed
from outside me into my bones,

up from the ground beneath me,
beneath this house, beneath
the road and the trees:

a silent delicate trembling no one has spoken of,
as if a beaten child or a captive animal
lay waiting the next blow.

It comes from the Earth herself, I tell you,
Earth herself. I whisper
because I'm ashamed. Isn't the earth our mother?
Isn't it we who've brought
this terror upon her?

Africa, gigantic slave-ship, not anchored yet not moving,
all hatches battened down, living tormented cargo
visible through dark but transparent sides. The sea
writhing too, but slowly, serpentine. In the vast hold,
vinelike hands reach out from crowded souls, strike sparks
from chains,

light fires in what space they make between their bodies:
not the ship only begins to burn,
the viscous depths it rides on

already smoulder.

A voice from the dark called out,
  'The poets must give us
imagination of peace, to oust the intense, familiar
imagination of disaster. Peace, not only
the absence of war.'
     But peace, like a poem,
is not there ahead of itself,
can't be imagined before it is made,
can't be known except
in the words of its making,
grammar of justice,
syntax of mutual aid.
    A feeling towards it,
dimly sensing a rhythm, is all we have
until we begin to utter its metaphors,
learning them as we speak.
     A line of peace might appear
if we restructured the sentence our lives are making,
revoked its reaffirmation of profit and power,
questioned our needs, allowed
long pauses . . .
    A cadence of peace might balance its weight
on that different fulcrum; peace, a presence,
an energy field more intense than war,
might pulse then,
stanza by stanza into the world,
each act of living
one of its words, each word
a vibration of light—facets
of the forming crystal.

From the Image-Flow—Summer of 1986

These days—these years—
when powers and principalities of death
weigh down the world, deeper, deeper
than we ever thought it could fall and still
                              keep slowly spinning,
Hope, caught under the jar's rim, crawls
like a golden fly
round and around, a sentinel:
it can't get out, it can't fly free
among our heavy hearts—
but does not die, keeps up its pace,
pausing only as if to meditate
a saving strategy . . .

V

SPINOFFS, TWO

'She wept, and the women consoled her.'

The flow of tears ebbed,
her blouse began to dry.
But the sobs that
took her by the shoulders and
shook her came back
for unknown reasons
and shook her again, like soldiers
coming back when everyone had gone.
History's traffic had speeded up and
smashed into gridlock all around her;
the women consoled her but she couldn't get out.
Bent forward as she was,
she found herself looking at her legs.
They were old, the skin
shiny over swollen ankles,
and blotched. They meant nothing to her
but they were all she could see.
Her fallen tears had left their traces
like snail-tracks on them.

'The day longs for the evening.'

The zenith longs for the banål horizon.
The north wind longs for the south,
and the trudging clouds are
searching, searching for that land
of glowing fruit, of polished marble;
but the wind that drives them
is bitter, they bring winter with them.
What is that promised evening?
The day, the day knows
in spite of everything,
that evening will not fail,
the ancient evening,
the luminous evening.

'The last heavy fairytale, in which one lays one's heart
bare before the knife.'

The room is small, the table plain,
white pine well-scrubbed.
The house is deep in the forest.
Each comes alone, but watched,
carefully holding in two hands
that heart which till now
was drumming and drumming away
in its own interior anteroom—
comes to center it, bare and still beating,
on the plain table
in the small room
where the knife will appear, new-sharpened, held
invisibly.

'The sea's repeated gesture.'

Stroking its blue shore
throughout the night, patient, patient,
determined rhetoric that never
persuades, the rocks unwilling
to be pebbles, nights and days and
centuries passing before the pebbles
dwindle to join the sand, the sand itself
at last barring the sea's way
into the land, an island
forming from the silt. Yet still
all this night and all
the nights of our life the sea
stroking its blue shore,
patient, patient—

'The myriad past, it enters us and disappears. Except
that within it somewhere, like diamonds, exist the frag-
ments that refuse to be consumed.'

Until sometimes an ancient
mind or body—it's not clear any more
which it may be—
those indurate insistences
having crowded out all else,
becomes all diamond:
hard transparence cut
to a thousand facets gleaming
with lights of the unseen,
a primal iridescence,
rainbow of death.

'The Holy One, blessed be he, wanders again,' said
Jacob, 'He is wandering and looks for a place where
he can rest.'

Between the pages
a wren's feather
to mark what passage?
Blood, not dry,
beaded scarlet on dusty stones.
A look of wonder
barely perceived on a turning face—
what, who had they seen?
Traces.
Here's the cold inn,
the wanderer passed it by
searching once more
for a stable's warmth,
a birthplace.

'I learned that her name was Proverb.'

And the secret names
of all we meet who lead us deeper
into our labyrinth
of valleys and mountains, twisting valleys
and steeper mountains—
their hidden names are always,
like Proverb, promises:
Rune, Omen, Fable, Parable,
those we meet for only
one crucial moment, gaze to gaze,
or for years know and don't recognize

but of whom later a word
sings back to us
as if from high among leaves,
still near but beyond sight

drawing us from tree to tree
towards the time and the unknown place
where we shall know
what it is to arrive.

VI

No one celebrates the allium.
The way each purposeful stem
ends in a globe, a domed umbel,
makes people think,
'Drumsticks', and that's that.
Besides, it's related to the onion.
Is that any reason
for disregard? The flowers—look—
are bouquets of miniature florets,
each with six elfin pointed petals
and some narrower ones my eyes
aren't sharp enough to count,
and three stamens about the size
of a long eyelash.
Every root
sends up a sheaf of sturdy
ridged stems, bounty
to fill your embrace. The bees
care for the allium, if you don't—
hear them now, doing their research,
humming the arias
of a honey opera, *Allium* it's called,
gold fur voluptuously
brushing that dreamy mauve.

Riding by taxi, Brooklyn to Queens,
a grey spring day. The Hispanic driver,
when I ask, 'Es usted Mexicano?' tells me
No, he's an exile from Uruguay. And I say,
'The only other Uruguayan I've met
was a writer—maybe
you know his name?—
                  Mario Benedetti?'
   And he takes both hands
off the wheel and swings round,
glittering with joy: '*Benedetti!*
Mario Benedetti!!'
                There are
hallelujas in his voice—
we execute a perfect
figure 8 on the shining highway,
and rise aloft, high above traffic, flying
all the rest of the way in the blue sky, azul, azul!

At sixteen I believed the moonlight
could change me if it would.
                    I moved my head
on the pillow, even moved my bed
as the moon slowly
crossed the open lattice.

I wanted beauty, a dangerous
gleam of steel, my body thinner,
my pale face paler.
                    I moonbathed
diligently, as others sunbathe.
But the moon's unsmiling stare
kept me awake. Mornings,
I was flushed and cross.

It was on dark nights of deep sleep
that I dreamed the most, sunk in the well,
and woke rested, and if not beautiful,
filled with some other power.

1   The Cherry Orchard

Not innocence; it was ignorance
lifted our chattering hoyden voices.
The orchard path, a shortcut to the village
where, when we got there, what was there to do?
—nothing to buy
but a handful of sticky sweets
our taste had outgrown.
Without mercy, without malice,
we tore off polished rubies, doubles and triples
of garnet baubles from the bent branches
to adorn our ears, wreathe in our Alice headbands,
devour. We spat the pale stones
from stained mouths, or from thumb and finger
flipped them to the treetops,
outscreaming the jays. We were indignant
when the farmer appeared
and raised his stick and shouted.
Our thieving troupe was beyond his reach.

Later, and older. Now we had suffered—a little.
When the way south became
a white road between fields of
fabled abundance, ranged in such weedless
elegance of order, we had no impulse, the two of us,
to trespass far into the serried vine;
but fruit nearest the verge we still thought
ours by right, to break our fast
as the dew vanished, the sun climbed. We slept
on bare ground, under stars, the nights of those days.

Not one by one but in passionate clusters
we pressed the grapes to our lips.
Their bloom was bloom,
the dust plain dust,
a time of happiness.
We had suffered
only a little, still,—our ignorance grown
only a little more shallow. There was something now
of innocence in us perhaps—we would not ask ourselves that
until we were almost old.

From the Image-Flow—Death of Chausson, 1899

Green in his mind the bows flicker, flicker and stream,
the piano's violet dapples the riverbed in arpeggios,
green, green the leaves.

Filled with summer his mind rises, his mind floats
a voice under branches, whisper of light, flying—
the leaves, the leaves:

and the road's long slope hums down to the shaded hollow,
a rushing scale, his wheels are spinning, his hat takes wing,
faster, faster, the brakes are asleep or deaf,
he is flying through green and violet
to the unseen wall, the silence.

Flickering curtain, scintillations, junebugs,
rain of fireflies low in the rippling fog,
motes abundant, random, pinpoints of intelligence
floating like bright snow . . .
A world, the world, where *live shell*
can explode on impact or, curled elaborate bone,
be an architecture, domicile
of wincing leisurely flesh.
                        The attention
sets out toward a cell, its hermit,
               the rapt years all one day,
                 telling and telling beads and vision—
        toward a river forever
        sweeping worn stones without impatience,
        holding its gesture, palm upraised—
but at once wavers: the shimmering curtain, wet strands
of hair, sound of the thick reeds jostled by what they hide,
life on the move, a caravan of event. Water an intermittent gleaming,
pools, marshes, a different river.

VII

All others talked as if
talk were a dance.
Clodhopper I, with clumsy feet
would break the gliding ring.
Early I learned to
hunch myself
close by the door:
then when the talk began
I'd wipe my
mouth and wend
unnoticed back to the barn
to be with the warm beasts,
dumb among body sounds
of the simple ones.
I'd see by a twist
of lit rush the motes
of gold moving
from shadow to shadow
slow in the wake
of deep untroubled sighs.
The cows
munched or stirred or were still. I
was at home and lonely,
both in good measure. Until
the sudden angel affrighted me—light effacing
my feeble beam,
a forest of torches, feathers of flame, sparks upflying:
but the cows as before
were calm, and nothing was burning,
            nothing but I, as that hand of fire
touched my lips and scorched my tongue
and pulled my voice
                    into the ring of the dance.

The Servant-Girl at Emmaus (A Painting by Velazquez)

She listens, listens, holding
her breath. Surely that voice
is his—the one
who had looked at her, once, across the crowd,
as no one ever had looked?
Had seen her? Had spoken as if to her?

Surely those hands were his,
taking the platter of bread from hers just now?
Hands he'd laid on the dying and made them well?

Surely that face—?

The man they'd crucified for sedition and blasphemy.
The man whose body disappeared from its tomb.
The man it was rumored now some women had seen this morning,
                                                    alive?

Those who had brought this stranger home to their table
don't recognize yet with whom they sit.
But she is in the kitchen, absently touching
                              the winejug she's to take in,
a young Black servant intently listening,

swings round and sees
the light around him
and is sure.

Assail God's hearing with gull-screech knifeblades.

Cozen the saints to plead our cause, claiming
grace abounding.

God crucified on the resolve not to displume
our unused wings

hears: nailed palms
cannot beat off the flames of insistent sound,

strident or plaintive,
nor reach to annul freedom—

nor would God renege.

Our shoulders ache. The abyss
gapes at us.

When shall we
dare to fly?

Six hours outstretched in the sun, yes,
hot wood, the nails, blood trickling
into the eyes, yes—
but the thieves on their neighbor crosses
survived till after the soldiers
had come to fracture their legs, or longer.
Why single out this agony? What's
a mere six hours?
Torture then, torture now,
the same, the pain's the same,
immemorial branding iron,
electric prod.
Hasn't a child
dazed in the hospital ward they reserve
for the most abused, known worse?
This air we're breathing,
these very clouds, ephemeral billows
languid upon the sky's
moody ocean, we share
with women and men who've held out
days and weeks on the rack—
and in the ancient dust of the world
what particles
of the long tormented,
what ashes.

But Julian's lucid spirit leapt
to the difference:
perceived why no awe could measure
that brief day's endless length,
why among all the tortured
One only is 'King of Grief'.
The oneing, she saw, *the oneing
with the Godhead* opened Him utterly
to the pain of all minds, all bodies

—sands of the sea, of the desert—
from first beginning
to last day. The great wonder is
that the human cells of His flesh and bone
didn't explode
when utmost Imagination rose
in that flood of knowledge. Unique
in agony, Infinite strength, Incarnate,
empowered Him to endure
inside of history,
through those hours when He took to Himself
the sum total of anguish and drank
even the lees of that cup:

within the mesh of the web, Himself
woven within it, yet seeing it,
seeing it whole. *Every sorrow and desolation*
He saw, and sorrowed in kinship.

With certitude
Simeon opened
ancient arms
to infant light.
Decades
before the cross, the tomb
and the new life,
he knew
new life.
What depth
of faith he drew on,
turning illumined
towards deep night.

Variation on a Theme by Rilke

(The Book of Hours, *Book I, Poem 4*)

All these images (said the old monk,
closing the book) these inspired depictions,
are true. Yes—not one—Giotto's,
Van Eyck's, Rembrandt's, Rouault's,
how many others'—
not one is a fancy, a willed fiction,
each of them shows us exactly
the manifold countenance
of the Holy One, Blessed be He.
The seraph buttress flying
to support a cathedral's external walls,
the shadowy ribs of the vaulted sanctuary:
aren't both—and equally—
the form of a holy place?—whose windows' ruby
and celestial sapphire can be seen
only from inside, but then
only when light enters from without?
From the divine twilight, neither dark nor day,
blossoms the morning. Each, at work in his art,
perceived his neighbor. Thus the Infinite
plays, and in grace
gives us clues to His mystery.

Be here:
surrounded
by stone,

by hewn stone, tints
of ochre, carnelian,

fieldstone graying
to dim white—

stones placed
one by one, a labor
arduous and exact.

Be here:
in presence
of stones, of silence,

of silence holding a pale
memory of shame,
of the cross
defiled (brandished
in war as a weapon)

of the poor
later, encamped
among charred
stones, time
of abandonment,
the altar fallen.

Be here:
where columns, arches
colors
of hay, of chaff,
of hedge-rose dust,
recall

the time of
stored grain, time
of sheep wintering,
drifted snow
heaped at
the broken door.

Be here, surrounded
by stone, by time,
by sunlight entering
like a bee at the
arched portal.

Here, where so long
no altar stood,
there stands, hewn
but not carved,
a block
of plain
stone unadorned,

and on the floor
before it, a gray
stoneware jar holds
(held, itself,
in the careful
space which
within the peace
of these ancient
stones
sustains us)

fading goldenrod,
fresh marguerites and
ardently pink
dahlias, dahlias
of bright
scarlet, dahlias
of garnet crimson,
almost black,
both reds
bloodred,

the entire bouquet
singing its colors
the livelong
empty day, the stones
resanctified.

The Showings: Lady Julian of Norwich, 1342–1416

1

Julian, there are vast gaps we call black holes,
unable to picture what's both dense and vacant;

and there's the dizzying multiplication of all
language can name or fail to name, unutterable
swarming of molecules. All Pascal
imagined he could not stretch his mind to imagine
is known to exceed his dread.

And there's the earth of our daily history,
its memories, its present filled with the grain
of one particular scrap of carpentered wood we happen
to be next to, its waking light on one especial leaf,
this word or that, a tune in this key not another,
beat of our hearts *now,* good or bad,
dying or being born, eroded, vanishing—

And you ask us to turn our gaze
inside out, and see
a little thing, the size of a hazelnut, and believe
it is our world? Ask us to see it lying
in God's pierced palm? That it encompasses
every awareness our minds contain? All Time?
All limitless space given form in this
medieval enigma?
                Yes, this is indeed
what you ask, sharing
the mystery you were shown: *all that is made:*
a little thing, the size of a hazelnut, held safe
in God's pierced palm.

What she petitioned for was never
instead of something else.
Thirty was older than it is now. She had not married
but was no starveling; if she had loved,
she had been loved. Death or some other destiny
bore him away, death or some other bride
changed him. Whatever that story,
long since she had travelled
through and beyond it. Somehow,
reading or read to, she'd spiralled
up within tall towers
of learning, steeples of discourse.
Bells in her spirit
rang new changes.
                Swept beyond event, one longing
outstripped all others: that reality,
supreme reality,
be witnessed. To desire wounds—
three, no less, no more—
is audacity, not, five centuries early, neurosis;
it's the desire to enact metaphor, for flesh to make known
to intellect (as uttered song
             makes known to voice,
            as image to eye)
make known in bone and breath
(and not die) God's agony.

3

'To understand her, you must imagine . . .'
A childhood, then;
the dairy's bowls of clabber, of rich cream,
ghost-white in shade, and outside
the midsummer gold, humming of dandelions.
To run back and forth, into the chill again,
the sweat of slate, a cake of butter
set on a green leaf—out once more
over slab of stone into hot light, hot
wood, the swinging gate!
A spire we think ancient split the blue
between two trees, a half-century old—
she thought it ancient.
Her father's hall, her mother's bower,
nothing was dull. The cuckoo
was changing its tune. In the church
there was glass in the windows, glass
colored like the world. You could see
Christ and his mother and his cross,
you could see his blood, and the throne of God.
In the fields
calves were lowing, the shepherd was taking the sheep
to new pasture.
                    Julian perhaps
not yet her name, this child's
that vivid woman.

4

God's wounded hand
reached out to place in hers
the entire world, 'round as a ball,
small as a hazelnut'. Just so one day
of infant light remembered
her mother might have given
into her two cupped palms
a newlaid egg, warm from the hen;
just so her brother
risked to her solemn joy
his delicate treasure,
a sparrow's egg from the hedgerow.
What can this be? *the eye of her understanding* marveled.

God for a moment in our history
placed in that five-fingered
human nest
the macrocosmic egg, sublime paradox,
brown hazelnut of All that Is—
made, and belov'd, and preserved.
As still, waking each day within
our microcosm, we find it, and ourselves.

Chapter Thirteen

Why did she laugh?
In scorn of malice.

What did they think?
They thought she was dying.

They caught her laugh?
Even the priest—

the dark small room
quivered with merriment,

all unaccountably
lightened.

If they had known
what she was seeing—

      the very
      spirit of evil,

      the Fiend they dreaded,
      seen to be oafish, ridiculous, vanquished—

what amazement! Stupid,
stupid his mar-plot malevolence!

Silly as his horns and
imaginary tail!

Why did her laughter
stop? Her mind moved on:

      the cost, the cost,
      the passion it took to undo

   the deeds of malice.
   The deathly

   wounds and the anguished
   heart.
And they?

They were abashed,
stranded in hilarity.

But when she recovered,
they told one another:

'Remember how we laughed
without knowing why?
That was the turning-point!'

6

Julian laughing aloud, glad
with *a most high inward happiness,*

Julian open calmly to dismissive judgements
flung backward down the centuries—
'delirium', 'hallucination';

Julian walking under-water
on the green hills of moss, the detailed sand and seaweed,
pilgrim of the depths, unfearing;

twenty years later carefully retelling
each unfading vision, each
pondered understanding;

Julian of whom we know
she had two serving-maids, Alice and Sara,
and kept a cat, and looked God in the face
and lived—

Julian nevertheless
said that *deeds are done so evil, injuries inflicted
so great, it seems to us
impossible any good
can come of them*—

any redemption, then, transform them . . .

She lived in dark times, as we do:
war, and the Black Death, hunger, strife,
torture, massacre. She knew
all of this, she felt it
*sorrowfully, mournfully,
shaken as men shake
a cloth in the wind.*

But Julian, Julian—
I turn to you:
you clung to joy though tears and sweat
rolled down your face like the blood
you watched pour down *in beads uncountable*
as rain from the eaves:
clung like an acrobat, by your teeth, fiercely,
to a cobweb-thin high-wire, your certainty
of infinite mercy, witnessed
with your own eyes, with outward sight
in your small room, with inward sight
in your untrammeled spirit—
knowledge we long to share:
Love was his meaning.

Variation and Reflection on a Theme by Rilke

(The Book of Hours, *Book I, Poem 7*)

1

If just for once the swing of cause and effect,
                  cause and effect,
would come to rest; if casual events would halt,
and the machine that supplies meaningless laughter
ran down, and my bustling senses, taking a deep breath
fell silent
and left my attention free at last . . .

then my thought, single and multifold,
could think you into itself
until it filled with you to the very brim,
bounding the whole flood of your boundlessness:

and at that timeless moment of possession,
fleeting as a smile, surrender you
and let you flow back into all creation.

2

There will never be that stillness.
Within the pulse of flesh,
in the dust of being, where we trudge,
      turning our hungry gaze this way and that,
the wings of the morning
brush through our blood
as cloud-shadows brush the land.
What we desire travels with us.
We must breathe time as fishes breathe water.
God's flight circles us.

Notes

3 'Variations on Themes by Rilke.' Those who read German will be able to see what images and ideas are taken from the original and which are my own. The proportions vary from poem to poem. (*Also see pages 71 and 83.*)

5 'August Daybreak.' The phrase 'a blissful foolish rose' is from 'A Ring of Changes' in *With Eyes at the Back of Our Heads* (New Directions, 1959).

6 'A Blessing.' Joanna Macy is the author of *Despair and Personal Power in the Nuclear Age*. 'The Council of All Beings' is a periodic gathering concerned with the concept of Deep Ecology.

9 'Spinoffs, First Group.' These 'span off' from photographs by Peter McAfee Brown when I was preparing to write an introduction to his work for a forthcoming publication. They should not be mistaken for descriptions.

33 'The Stricken Children.' Originally titled 'In Thatcher's England, 1985.' That title was appropriate but—alas—too restrictive.

36 'Carapace.' This draws on a PBS *Frontline* program on El Salvador.

40 'Making Peace.' 'The imagination of disaster' is Henry James's phrase. He said Americans had it—but do they still? Imagination is what makes reality real to the mind (which is why it's so hard to imagine peace, for it has not been experienced in the reality of our life in history except as the absence of war). Yet not only peace but the disastrous realities of our time go unimagined, even when 'known about,' when 'psychic numbing' veils them; and thus the energy to act constructively, which *imaginative* knowledge could generate, is repressed.

43 'Spinoffs, Second Group.' In the same way that the poems of 'Spinoffs, First Group,' 'span off' from photographs, these did so from sentences, taken out of context, in what I happened to be reading at the time—Ernst Wiechert, James Salter, others I have forgotten. The exact sources are not relevant to the poems except in one case, 'I learned that her name was Proverb,' which comes from the dream which Thomas Merton recounted in a letter to Boris Pasternak (quoted in a review by Father Basil Pennington of Michael Mott's biography of Thomas Merton (*National Catholic Reporter,* January 11, 1985)). The letter which is alluded to by Mott is in the Thomas Merton Studies center at Bellarmine, Kentucky. The poems are not a sequence, i.e., their order is arbitrary. A 'spinoff,' then, is a verbal construct which neither

85

describes nor comments but moves off at a tangent to, or parallel with, its inspiration.

60 'Death of Chausson.' Ernest Chausson, composer, 1855–1899.

65 'Caedmon.' The story comes, of course, from The Venerable Bede's *History of the the English Church and People,* but I first read it as a child in John Richard Green's *History of the English People,* 1855. The poem forms a companion piece to 'St. Peter and the Angel' in *Oblique Prayers.*

66 'The Servant-Girl at Emmaus.' The painting is in the collection at Russborough House, County Wicklow, Ireland. Before it was cleaned, the subject was not apparent: only when the figures at table in a room behind her were revealed was her previously ambiguous expression clearly legible as acutely attentive.

68 'On a Theme from Julian's Chapter XX.' This is from the longer text of Julian of Norwich's *Showings* (or *Revelations*). The quoted lines follow the Grace Warrack transcription (1901). Warrack uses the word 'kinship' in her title-heading for the chapter, though in the text itself she says 'kindness,' thus—as in her Glossary—reminding one of the roots common to both words.

70 'Candlemas.' This draws on a sermon given by Father Benignus at Stanford, Candlemas 1985.

72 'La Cordelle.' A small chapel on the hillside below Vézelay.

75 'The Showings.' The quotations are taken from the *Pelican* and the *Classics of Western Spirituality* editions.